LONG AGO and TODAY

A City Album

Peter and Connie Roop

Heinemann Library
Des Plaines, Illinois

© 1999 Reed Educational & Professional Publishing
Published by Heinemann Library,
an imprint of Reed Educational & Professional Publishing,
1350 East Touhy Avenue, Suite 240 West
Des Plaines, IL 60018

Designed by Lindaanne Donohoe
Printed in Hong Kong

03 02 01 00
10 9 8 7 6 5 4 3

Library of Congress Cataloging-in-Publication Data
Roop, Peter
     A City album / Peter and Connie Roop.
        p.   cm. — (Long ago and today)
     Includes bibliographical references and index.
     Summary: Text, photographs, and illustrations identify and trace
patterns of continuity and change in cities in the United States,
including such topics as transportation, homes, recreation, and
employment.
     ISBN 1-57572-600-9 (lib. bdg.)
     1. Cities and towns—United States— Juvenile literature. 2. City
and town life—United States—History—Juvenile literature. (1.Cities and
towns. 2. City and town life.) I. Roop, Connie. II. Title.
III. Series: Roop, Peter. Long ago and today.
HT123.R64724   1998
307.76'0973—dc21
                                                                    98-15553
                                                                       CIP
                                                                        AC

Acknowledgments
The authors and publishers are grateful to the following for permission to reproduce
copyright photographs:
Cover photographs: Stock Montage, Inc., top; Phil Martin, bottom
Corbis-Bettmann, pp. 4, 6, 10, 14, 16, 22 top, back cover right; Stock Montage, Inc., pp.12, 18,
20; Chicago Historical Society, p. 8; Steve Benbow, p. 13; Darren Yokota, pp. 5, 7 top, 22
bottom; Graham Gordon Ramsay, p. 15; Phil Martin, pp. 7 bottom, 9, 11,17, 19, 21, back cover
left.

Every effort has been made to contact copyright holders of any material reproduced in this
book. Any omissions will be rectified in subsequent printings if notice is given to the publisher.

Some words are shown in bold, **like this.** You can find out what they mean by looking
in the glossary.

For Jane—in appreciation for your friendship and team spirit.
          Working with you is always a pleasure.

Contents

The City

Mulberry Street, New York City, 1897

A long time ago, there were few big cities in the United States. Most people lived on farms or in **villages** and small towns. There were fewer people than there are today.

Today, most Americans live in or near a big city. Few people live on farms or in small towns. There are now nearly 265 million people living in the United States. People from around the world live in the United States.

Mulberry Street, New York City, 1998

Places to Live

Cannon Street, New York City, 1890

Long ago, cities were busy but not too crowded. There were no elevators so buildings were only one or two stories tall. People lived in houses in the cities. There was no electricity. Homes and streets were lit with candles and lamps.

Today, cities are busy and crowded. Buildings can be very tall because elevators carry people up high. Some buildings have fifty stories or more. Most people live in tall apartment buildings where many other families live. Apartments, homes, and streets are brightly lit with electric lights.

two kinds of tall city buildings, 1998

Getting Around

South Water Street, Chicago, 1871

People long ago walked or rode horses in cities. Cities were small and easy to get around. Streets were wide. Sometimes they were paved with stones or bricks. Many streets were just dirt. They were dusty when dry and muddy when wet.

Today, people get around in cities in cars. Many ride in cabs. Others ride buses or **subways.** City streets are crowded with trucks, cars, cabs, buses, bicycles, and people walking. City streets are paved.

St. Charles Avenue, New Orleans, 1998

Trains and Trolleys

Long ago, if people had to travel across the city, they rode in a wagon or a **trolley** pulled by a horse. Some cities had railroads. City streets were noisy with animals running loose, horses neighing, and people talking.

San Francisco cable car, 1880

Chicago elevated train, 1998

Buses, **subways,** and **elevated trains** carry people into and around cities today. Railroads bring people and products into the city. Streets are noisy with cars honking, machines working, sirens screaming, trains and trucks rolling, and people talking.

Food

general store, 1885

Long ago, people in cities kept animals for food. Cows gave milk for cheese and butter. Chickens gave eggs. Ham and bacon came from hogs. Families also grew potatoes, onions, beans, and cabbage. Families baked their own bread. General stores sold food and other things people needed.

Today, people in cities keep animals as pets. Some people grow food in tiny gardens. City people buy their food at grocery stores or small shops. Fresh food is shipped into the city each morning. Different foods can be bought in different shops—meat in a **deli,** bread in a bakery, vegetables at a **stall.** Restaurants serve foods from around the world.

city grocery store, 1997

Parks

Boston Common in the 1800s

Long ago, there were no parks in cities. There were **meadows,** woods, and ponds. As more people moved into cities, these areas were filled with buildings. People started saving space for parks.

Cities today have many parks. Some parks are large and have ponds, trees, and playing fields. Others are small with a few bushes and trees. People in cities need parks for fun and rest.

Boston Common, 1998

Schools

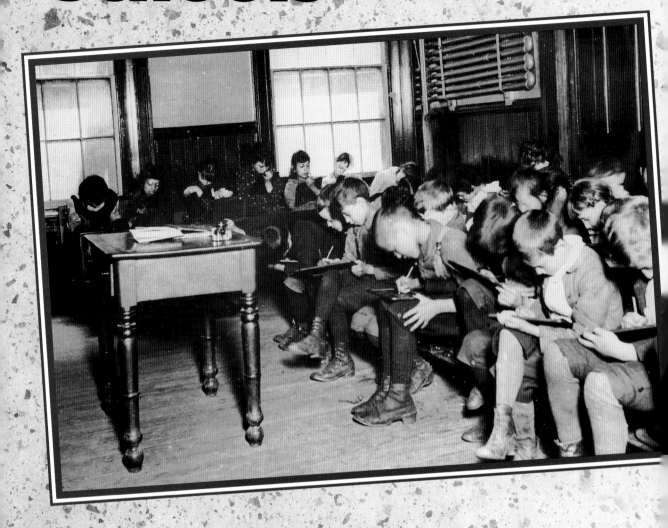

public school, 1892

Long ago, not all children in cities went to school. Some went to small schools for just boys or girls. Others went to school from first to eighth grade. Most children helped with chores at home or did jobs to make money for their families.

Today, city children go to school. Some schools are small. Others are very large and crowded. Children go to school from kindergarten to high school. Many help at home or do jobs after school.

public school, 1998

Playing

Long ago in cities, there were no basketball, football, or hockey teams. People played baseball or **stickball.** They walked and talked together. Children played games in the streets or fields.

playing on the swings in the park, 1871

playing basketball in a gym, 1998

Today, many big cities have professional sports teams. Players get paid to play baseball, basketball, football, and hockey. Children and adults play baseball, basketball, soccer, and other games in playgrounds, parks, and gyms.

Where People Work

city blacksmith's shop

People long ago worked in shops and factories in cities. Many people also worked at home. They made small things like buttons, needles, matches, or clothes. They walked or rode horses or **trolleys** to work.

Today, many people still work in shops and factories. Others work in tall office buildings. Many city workers live outside the city and drive or ride trains, **subways,** and buses to work in the city.

city office, 1998

Cities Long Ago and Today

The same city street in 1900 and 1998. What is the same? What has changed?

People long ago lived, worked, and played in cities just as people do today. But many things are different. Homes, **transportation**, and jobs are much different today. These differences have changed the way people in cities live.

Glossary

blacksmith person who works with iron to make horseshoes

deli small shop that sells meats, fish, cheese, and salads

elevated trains trains that run on tracks built above city streets

meadows large fields

stall small shop in an outdoor market where people sell things

stickball game like baseball using a stick instead of a bat to hit a ball

subways trains that run on tracks underground

transportation ways people travel

trolley streetcar pulled by horses

villages very small towns

More Books to Read

Brown, Craig. *City Sounds.* New York: Greenwillow Books, 1992.

Llewellyn, Claire. *Cities.* Des Plaines, Ill: Heinemann Library, 1997.

Ask an older reader to help you read this book: Kalman, Bobbi. *Early City Life.* New York: Crabtree Publishing, 1983.

Index